Magical Maths

Lynn Huggins-Cooper

Wizard Whimstaff lives in a faraway land, in a magical cave. He searches for apprentices so he can pass on his powerful Maths spells. And this time Wizard Whimstaff has chosen you!

He has a goblin helper called Pointy, who is very clever. Pointy helps Wizard Whimstaff keep his spell books tidy. He also stirs the smelly cauldron to make numbers appear.

Pointy has two pet frogs called Mugly and Bugly. They are very lazy. They spend most of their time eating, burping and sleeping. Their friend Miss Snufflebeam also lives in the cave. She is a small dragon. She cannot breathe fire yet, so puffs little clouds of smoke instead!

Wizard Whimstaff and his friends are very happy, solving Maths problems. Join them on a magical quest to win the Trophy of Maths Wizardry!

Contents

2	Nifty Numbers	18	Halving and Doubling
4	Magical Ordering	20	Spooky Shapes
6	Terrifying Tens	22	Amazing Addition
8	Wonderful Words	24	Silly Subtraction
10	**More** and **Less** Wizardry	26	Super Sizes
12	Toady Tens	28	Apprentice Wizard Challenge 2
14	Apprentice Wizard Challenge 1	30	Answers
16	Beastly Bonds	32	Wizard's Trophy of Excellence

Letts

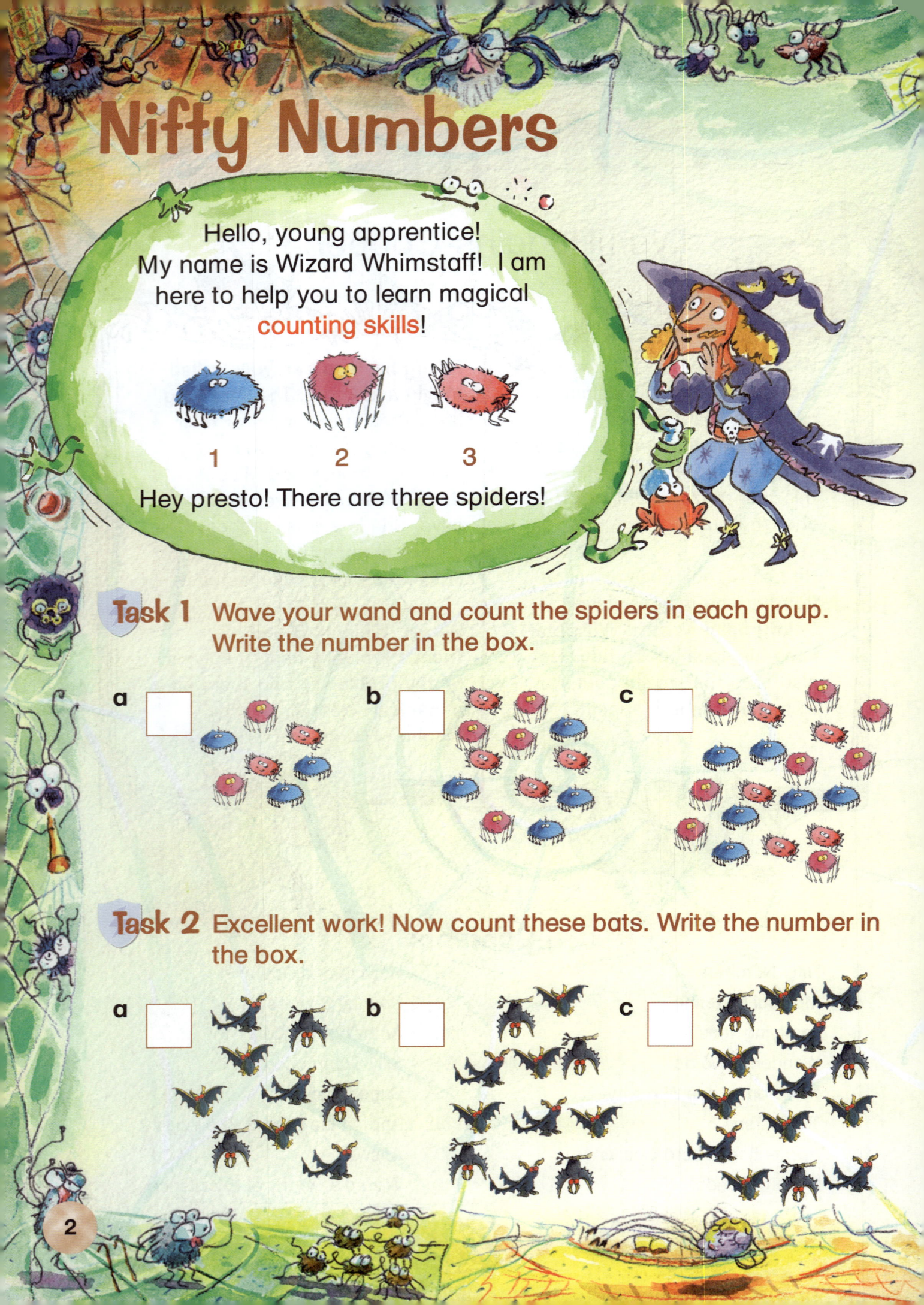

Nifty Numbers

Hello, young apprentice! My name is Wizard Whimstaff! I am here to help you to learn magical **counting skills**!

1   2   3

Hey presto! There are three spiders!

Task 1 Wave your wand and count the spiders in each group. Write the number in the box.

a ☐   b ☐   c ☐

Task 2 Excellent work! Now count these bats. Write the number in the box.

a ☐   b ☐   c ☐

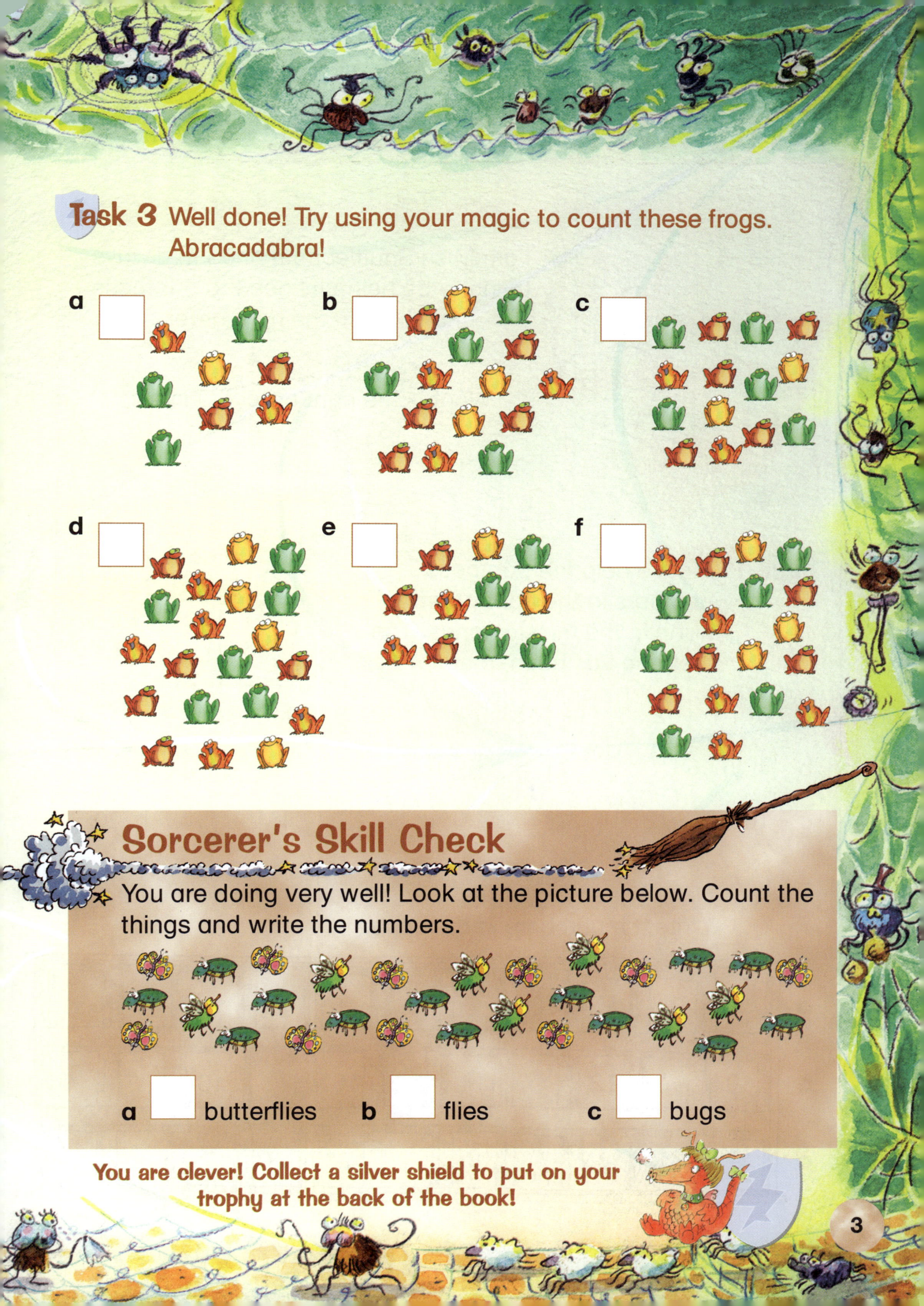

Task 3 Well done! Try using your magic to count these frogs. Abracadabra!

a ☐

b ☐

c ☐

d ☐

e ☐

f ☐

Sorcerer's Skill Check

You are doing very well! Look at the picture below. Count the things and write the numbers.

a ☐ butterflies   b ☐ flies   c ☐ bugs

You are clever! Collect a silver shield to put on your trophy at the back of the book!

3

Magical Ordering

I am Miss Snufflebeam and I'm always trying to be helpful! I need to put these numbers in the right order.

3 5 2 1 4

What is the right order? Oh yes!

1 2 3 4 5

> 1 2 3 4 5
> 6 7 8 9 10
> 11 12 13 14 15
> 16 17 18 19 20

Task 1 Please help me put these numbers in the right order by filling in the missing ones. The first one has been done for us.

a 0 [1] 2 3 [4] 5 6 [7] 8 9 10

b 4 5 6 [ ] [ ] [ ] 10 [ ] [ ] [ ]

c 10 11 12 [ ] [ ] [ ] [ ] [ ] [ ] 20

Task 2 Help! I need to put these spellbooks in the right order. Write the numbers in the gaps.

a 3 [ ] 5 [ ] [ ] 8 9

b 10 [ ] 12 [ ] 14 [ ] 16 [ ] 18 [ ] 20

c 1 [ ] 3 [ ] 5 [ ] 7 8 9

4

Task 3 I am going to sing some happy number songs. Help me to fill in the numbers as I sing!

a 1 ___ 3 ___ 5, once I caught a bat alive!

b 6 ___ 8 ___ 10, then I let her go again!

c 1 ___ ___ ___ 5, then I caught a toad alive!

d 6 ___ ___ ___ 10, then I let him go again!

Why did I let them go? Mugly slurped my finger so!

Which finger did he slurp? This one, then he did a burp!

e 1 ___, Pointy made some stew,

f 3 ___, I spilled it on the floor!

g ___ 6, the Wizard did some tricks,

h ___ ___, they were really great!

Sorcerer's Skill Check

You are so clever! Fill in the missing numbers.

a 9 10 ☐ ☐ ☐ ☐ ☐

b 7 ☐ ☐ 10 11 ☐ ☐

c 12 ☐ ☐ ☐ ☐ ☐ ☐ 19 20

d 2 ☐ ☐ ☐ 6 7 8 ☐ ☐

Well done! You can add a silver shield to your trophy! Super!

Terrifying Tens

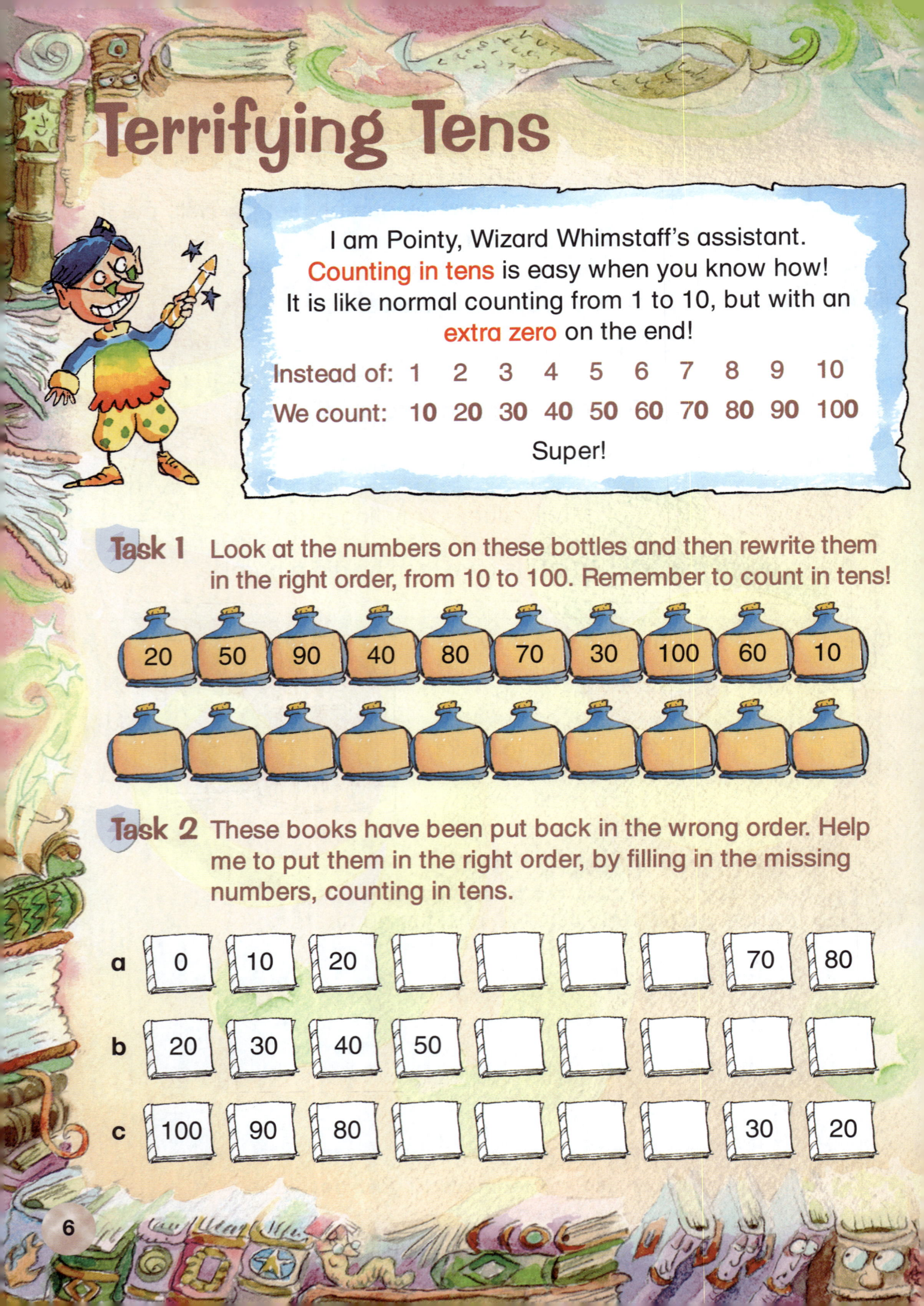

I am Pointy, Wizard Whimstaff's assistant. **Counting in tens** is easy when you know how! It is like normal counting from 1 to 10, but with an **extra zero** on the end!

Instead of: 1   2   3   4   5   6   7   8   9   10
We count: **10 20 30 40 50 60 70 80 90 100**

Super!

Task 1 Look at the numbers on these bottles and then rewrite them in the right order, from 10 to 100. Remember to count in tens!

20 50 90 40 80 70 30 100 60 10

Task 2 These books have been put back in the wrong order. Help me to put them in the right order, by filling in the missing numbers, counting in tens.

a | 0 | 10 | 20 | | | | 70 | 80 |

b | 20 | 30 | 40 | 50 | | | | |

c | 100 | 90 | 80 | | | | 30 | 20 |

Task 3 Now see if you can put these frogs in order on a numberline, starting from 100 and counting down in tens to zero! Write the correct order on the numberline below.

70 0 30 20 10
50 60 90
100 80 40

Sorcerer's Skill Check

Finally, use your magic to fill in the numberline on the stars, counting in tens from 0 to 70!

0

Burp! Well done, clever clogs! Collect a silver shield for your trophy!

Wonderful Words

We are Mugly and Bugly, the two lazy frogs! Now, frogs change from small tadpoles to grown-up frogs. But numbers are far more confusing! They can be changed from numbers to words and then changed back to numbers again. To become as clever as Wizard Whimstaff, you need to be able to write numbers **and** words.

1   one

Task 1 Help us match the numbers to the words that mean the same! We have done the first one, but now we are off for a snooze.

2 7 0 4 10 9 5 3 8 1 6

nine   four   ten   five   six

one   seven   eight   three   two   zero

Task 2 Slurp! We need a snack now. Write the numbers on the spiders to match the words shown. Then we can eat them in the right order!

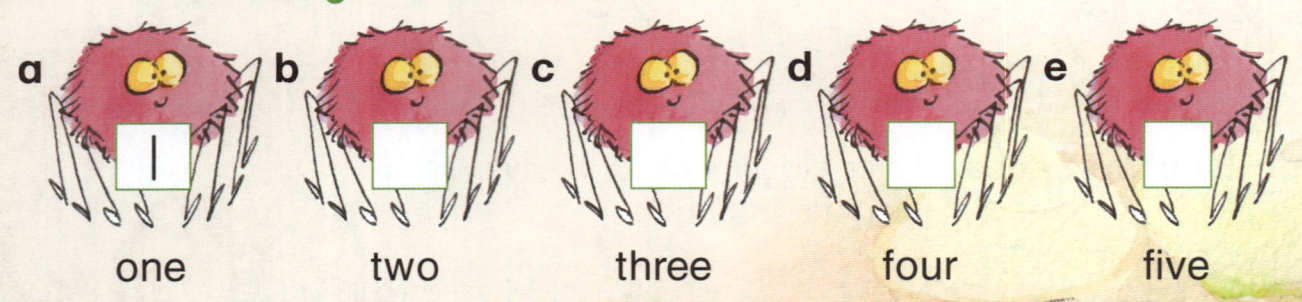

a. 1 — one
b. ☐ — two
c. ☐ — three
d. ☐ — four
e. ☐ — five

Task 3 We need to put our frog food in the right order! Then we will know which one to eat first! Can you help us? Write the letters in the boxes below to show the right order.

a. Fat frog food four
b. Fat frog food six
c. Fat frog food one
d. Fat frog food three
e. Fat frog food two
f. Fat frog food five

[c] [ ] [ ] [ ] [ ] [ ]

Task 4 Slurp! Delicious work! Now write the numbers on each of these spiders out in words below.

a. 10
b. 1
c. 2
d. 3
e. 6

Sorcerer's Skill Check

Croak! Check what you have learnt so far! Match the numbers on the frogs to the words on the lily pads. The first one has been done for you.

a. 10
b. 3
c. 8
d. 1
e. 7
f. 9
g. 2
h. 6
i. 0
j. 4
k. 5

ten   zero   seven   nine   two
three   four   eight   one   five   six

You are a wonderful word wizard! Give yourself another silver shield!

9

More and Less Wizardry

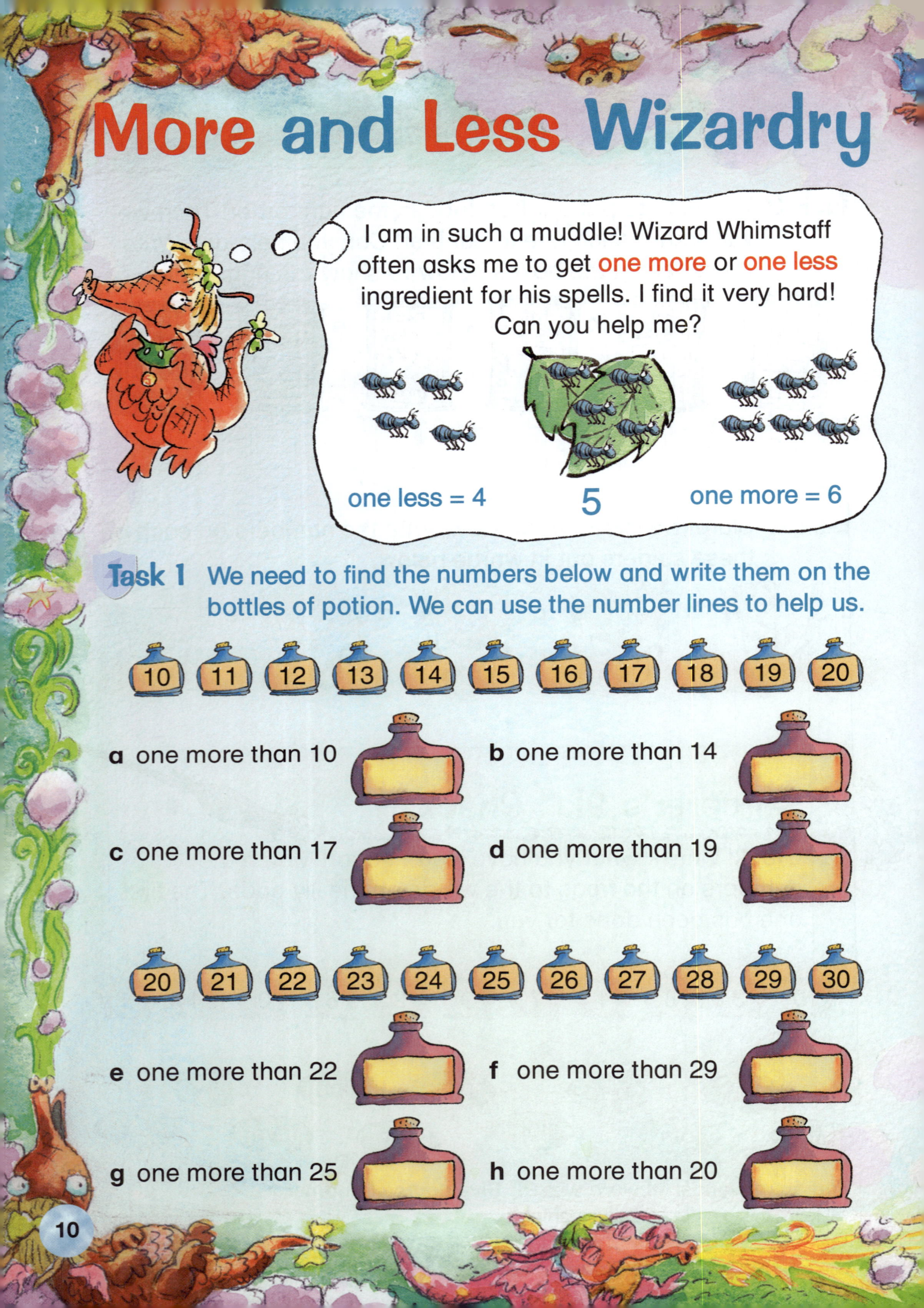

I am in such a muddle! Wizard Whimstaff often asks me to get **one more** or **one less** ingredient for his spells. I find it very hard! Can you help me?

one less = 4   5   one more = 6

Task 1 We need to find the numbers below and write them on the bottles of potion. We can use the number lines to help us.

10 11 12 13 14 15 16 17 18 19 20

a one more than 10
b one more than 14
c one more than 17
d one more than 19

20 21 22 23 24 25 26 27 28 29 30

e one more than 22
f one more than 29
g one more than 25
h one more than 20

Task 2 Now use your magic to find these numbers.

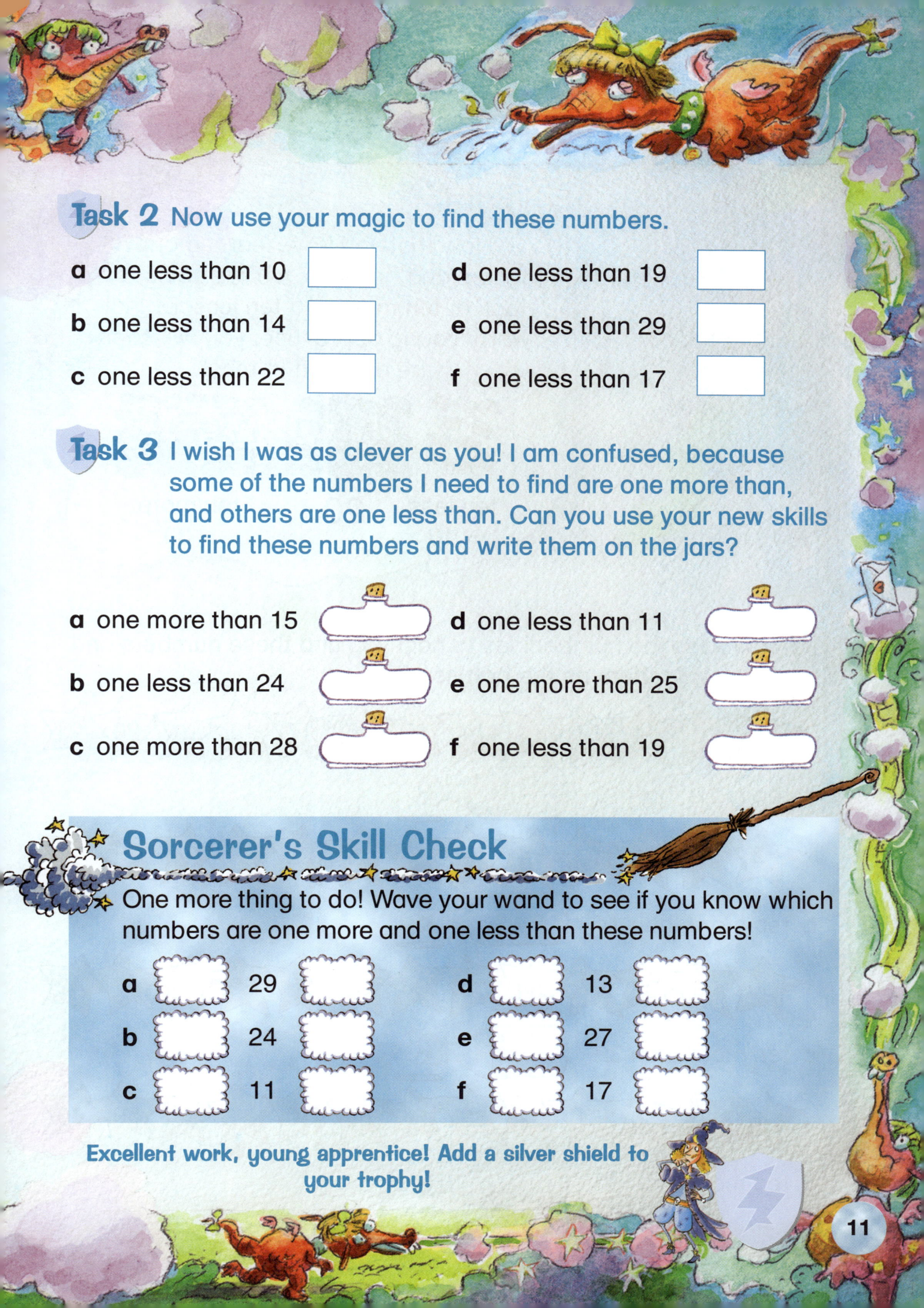

a one less than 10

b one less than 14

c one less than 22

d one less than 19

e one less than 29

f one less than 17

Task 3 I wish I was as clever as you! I am confused, because some of the numbers I need to find are one more than, and others are one less than. Can you use your new skills to find these numbers and write them on the jars?

a one more than 15

b one less than 24

c one more than 28

d one less than 11

e one more than 25

f one less than 19

Sorcerer's Skill Check

One more thing to do! Wave your wand to see if you know which numbers are one more and one less than these numbers!

a ☐ 29 ☐

b ☐ 24 ☐

c ☐ 11 ☐

d ☐ 13 ☐

e ☐ 27 ☐

f ☐ 17 ☐

Excellent work, young apprentice! Add a silver shield to your trophy!

Toady Tens

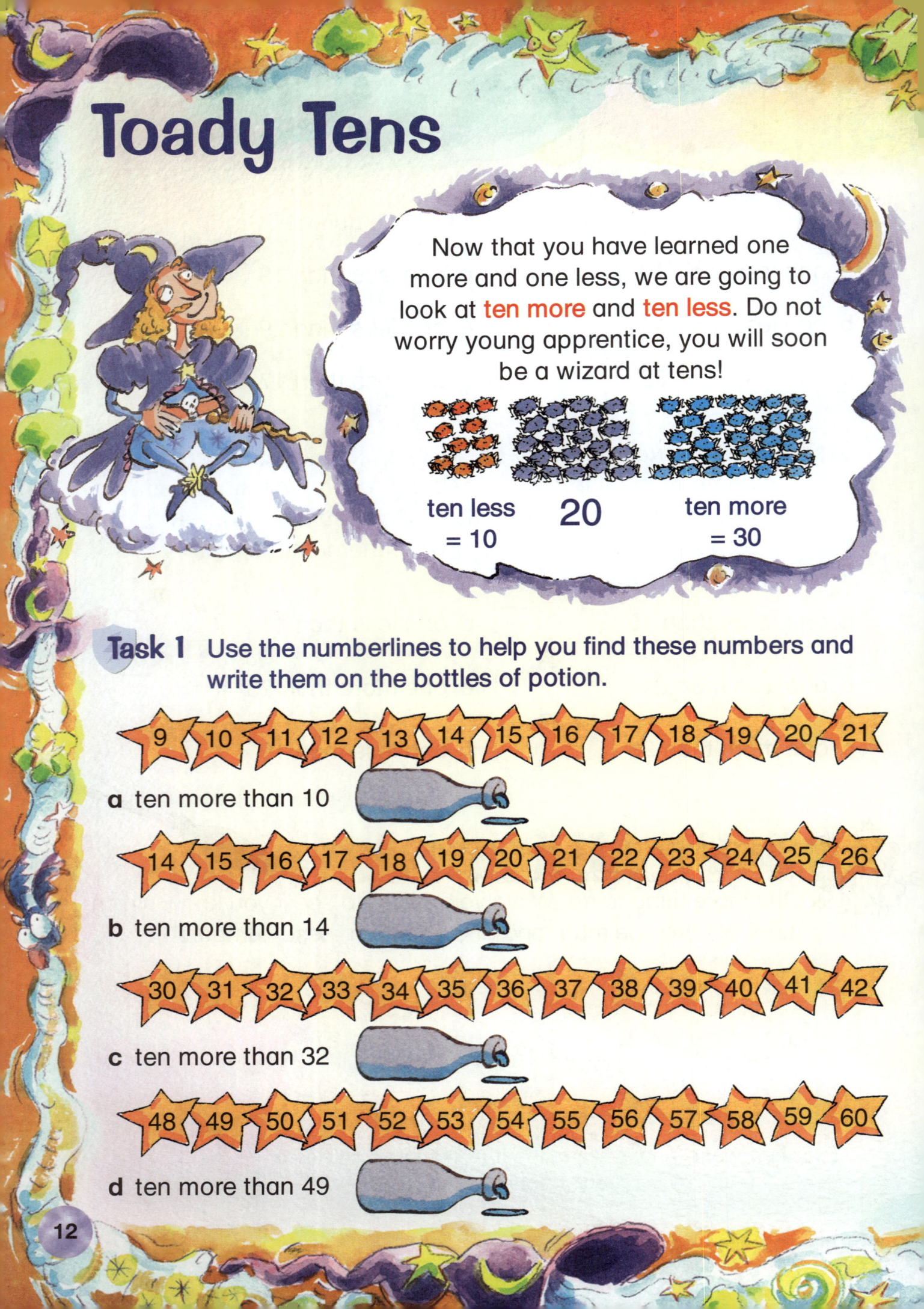

Now that you have learned one more and one less, we are going to look at **ten more** and **ten less**. Do not worry young apprentice, you will soon be a wizard at tens!

ten less = 10   20   ten more = 30

Task 1 Use the numberlines to help you find these numbers and write them on the bottles of potion.

9 10 11 12 13 14 15 16 17 18 19 20 21

a ten more than 10

14 15 16 17 18 19 20 21 22 23 24 25 26

b ten more than 14

30 31 32 33 34 35 36 37 38 39 40 41 42

c ten more than 32

48 49 50 51 52 53 54 55 56 57 58 59 60

d ten more than 49

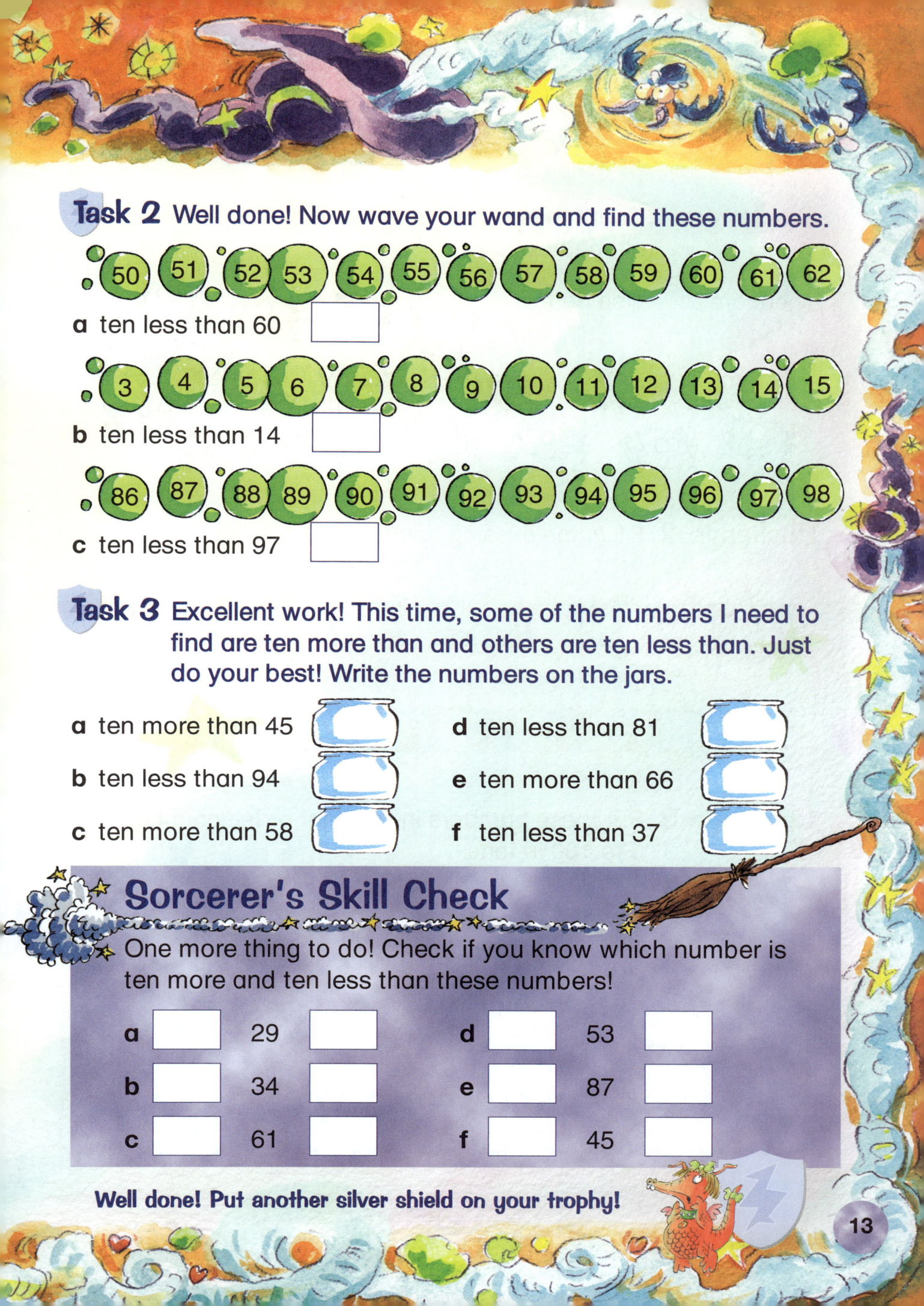

Task 2 Well done! Now wave your wand and find these numbers.

50 51 52 53 54 55 56 57 58 59 60 61 62

a ten less than 60 ☐

3 4 5 6 7 8 9 10 11 12 13 14 15

b ten less than 14 ☐

86 87 88 89 90 91 92 93 94 95 96 97 98

c ten less than 97 ☐

Task 3 Excellent work! This time, some of the numbers I need to find are ten more than and others are ten less than. Just do your best! Write the numbers on the jars.

a ten more than 45
b ten less than 94
c ten more than 58

d ten less than 81
e ten more than 66
f ten less than 37

Sorcerer's Skill Check

One more thing to do! Check if you know which number is ten more and ten less than these numbers!

a ☐ 29 ☐   d ☐ 53 ☐
b ☐ 34 ☐   e ☐ 87 ☐
c ☐ 61 ☐   f ☐ 45 ☐

Well done! Put another silver shield on your trophy!

Apprentice Wizard Challenge 1

Challenge 1 Count these spiders. How many are there altogether?

There are ☐ spiders

Challenge 2 Fill in the missing numbers.

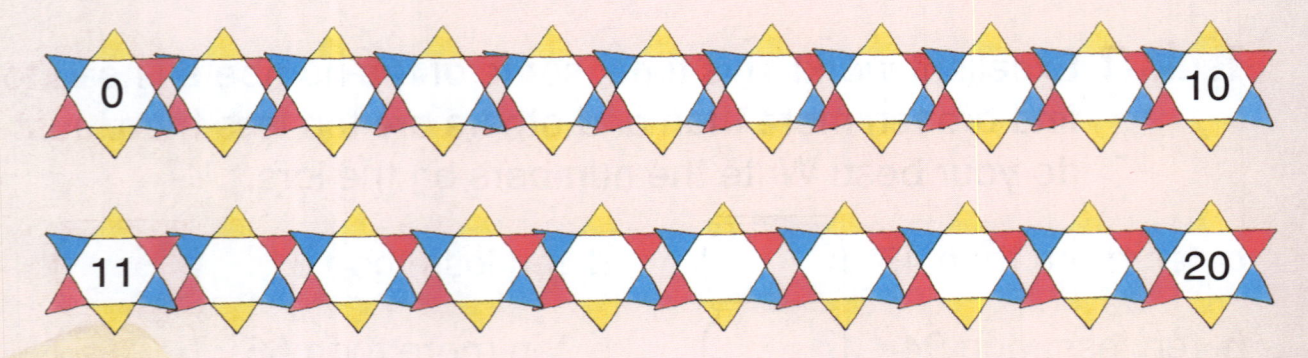

0 ... 10

11 ... 20

Challenge 3 Put these numbers in the right order, counting from 0 to 100 in tens.

80 20 40 90 50 70

30 60 0 100 10

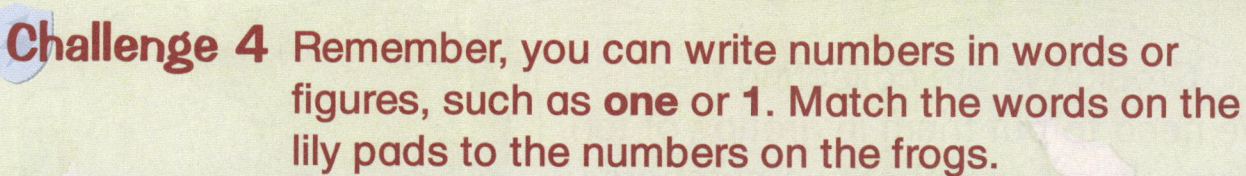

Challenge 4 Remember, you can write numbers in words or figures, such as **one** or **1**. Match the words on the lily pads to the numbers on the frogs.

Lily pads: six, two, four, three, five, ten
Frogs: 10, 5, 3, 4, 6, 2

Challenge 5 Check if you know which number is one more and one less than these numbers!

a ☐ 29 ☐
b ☐ 24 ☐
c ☐ 11 ☐

d ☐ 13 ☐
e ☐ 27 ☐
f ☐ 17 ☐

Challenge 6 Check if you know which number is ten more and ten less than these numbers!

a ☐ 49 ☐
b ☐ 84 ☐
c ☐ 91 ☐

d ☐ 55 ☐
e ☐ 71 ☐
f ☐ 45 ☐

Put stars on the test tube to show your challenge score. Then have a silver shield for your trophy!

Beastly Bonds

Croak! We are collecting flies. We need to put them in **groups of ten**. When we put together two numbers to make ten we say they are **number bonds** that make ten.

5 + 5 = 10

Task 1 Burp! These flies look tasty! Match the swarms of flies to make groups of ten.

a   b   c   d   e

Task 2 Grub's up! Now we have groups of spiders to sort. Can you match the gangs of spiders to make groups of ten?

a   b   c   d   e

16

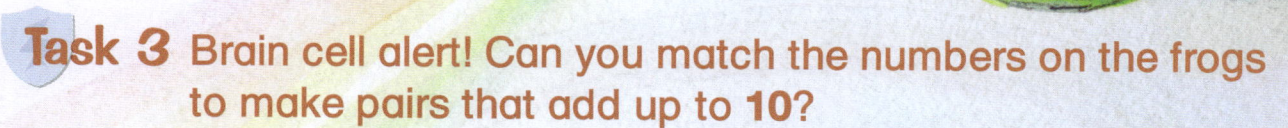

Task 3 Brain cell alert! Can you match the numbers on the frogs to make pairs that add up to **10**?

a 3   b 0   c 9   d 8   e 6   f 5

1   2   5   7   10   4

Sorcerer's Skill Check

This must be a job for Pointy! But see if you can do it. Use your magic to conjure up the missing numbers.

a 0 + ⬡ = 10   **g** 6 + ⬡ = 10

b 1 + ⬡ = 10   **h** 7 + ⬡ = 10

c 2 + ⬡ = 10   **i** 8 + ⬡ = 10

d 3 + ⬡ = 10   **j** 9 + ⬡ = 10

e 4 + ⬡ = 10   **k** 10 + ⬡ = 10

f 5 + ⬡ = 10

You will be as clever as Wizard Whimstaff soon! Another silver shield for your trophy!

Halving and Doubling

Pointy here again! Wizard Whimstaff has asked me to test his amazing halving and doubling potions! When I use them on these frogs, the frogs double or half. Super!

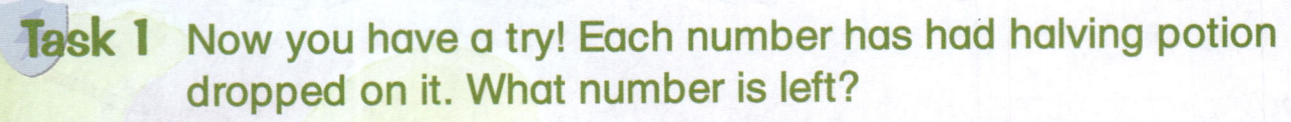

half of 🐸🐸🐸🐸 = 🐸🐸

double of 🐸🐸🐸 = 🐸🐸🐸🐸🐸🐸

Task 1 Now you have a try! Each number has had halving potion dropped on it. What number is left?

a half 4 = ☐ b half 6 = ☐

c half 8 = ☐ d half 2 = ☐

Task 2 It is easy when you know how! This time, each number has had doubling potion dropped on it. What number is made?

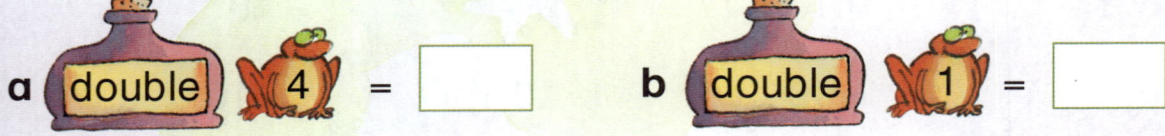

a double 4 = ☐ b double 1 = ☐

c double 2 = ☐ d double 3 = ☐

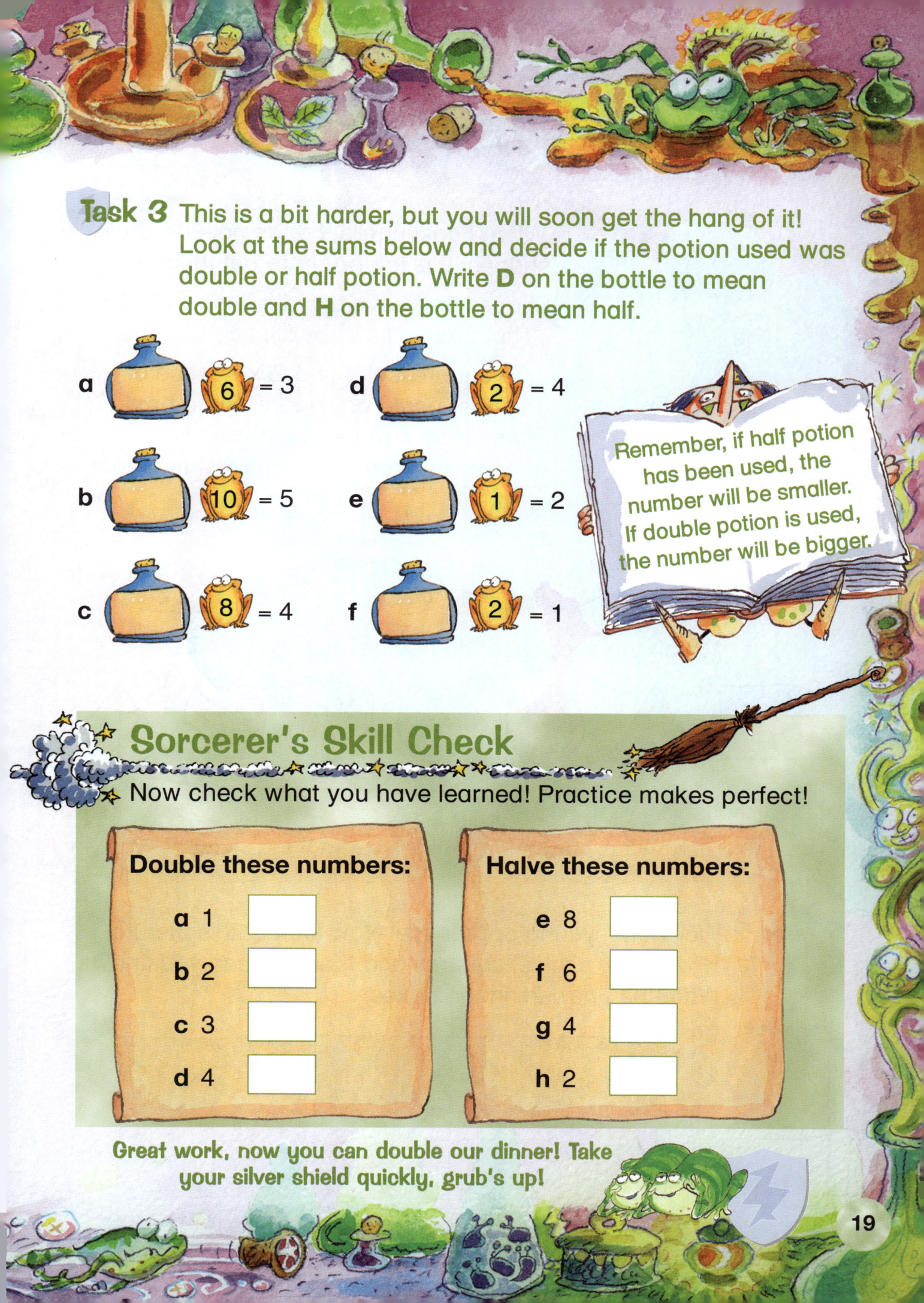

Task 3 This is a bit harder, but you will soon get the hang of it! Look at the sums below and decide if the potion used was double or half potion. Write **D** on the bottle to mean double and **H** on the bottle to mean half.

a   6 = 3

b   10 = 5

c   8 = 4

d   2 = 4

e   1 = 2

f   2 = 1

Remember, if half potion has been used, the number will be smaller. If double potion is used, the number will be bigger.

Sorcerer's Skill Check

Now check what you have learned! Practice makes perfect!

Double these numbers:

a 1

b 2

c 3

d 4

Halve these numbers:

e 8

f 6

g 4

h 2

Great work, now you can double our dinner! Take your silver shield quickly, grub's up!

19

Spooky Shapes

When I cast spells, I often need to draw **shapes**. It is important to get them right.

Shapes can be in two dimensions or **2D**. That means flat, like a piece of paper.

A square is flat and 2D. A piece of paper could be square. But a box, made from squares, is **3D** and is called a cube. You can put things inside a box!

Task 1 Match the shapes to the names. Just do your best!

a   b   c   d   e   f   g

circle • square • pyramid • sphere • triangle • hexagon • cube

Task 2 Well done, young apprentice! Now look at this picture. How many circles, squares and triangles can you find? Write the answers in the boxes.

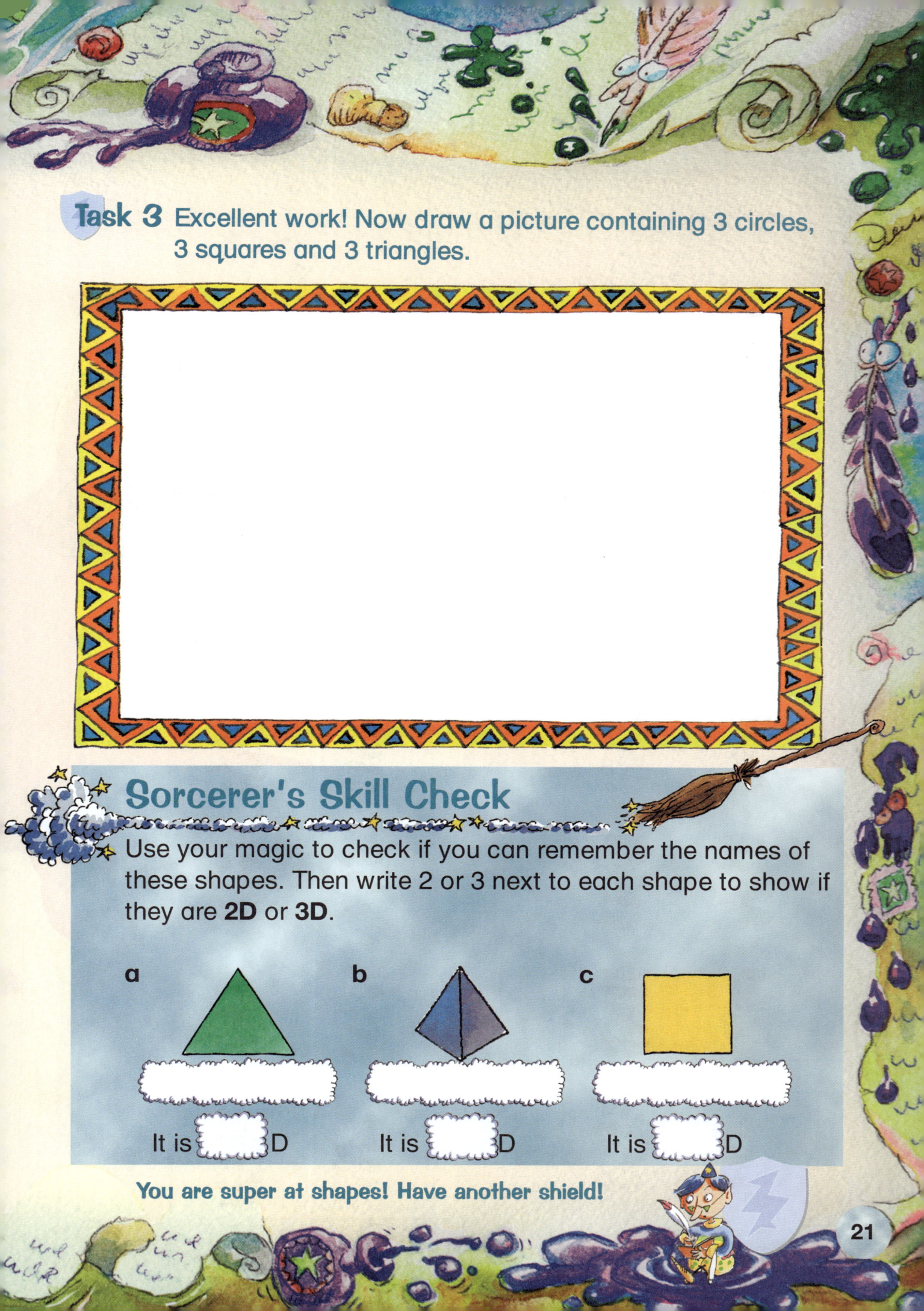

Task 3 Excellent work! Now draw a picture containing 3 circles, 3 squares and 3 triangles.

Sorcerer's Skill Check

Use your magic to check if you can remember the names of these shapes. Then write 2 or 3 next to each shape to show if they are **2D** or **3D**.

a

b

c

It is ___D   It is ___D   It is ___D

You are super at shapes! Have another shield!

Amazing Addition

Slurp! Mugly and Bugly here again! We are a bit tired, but we need to tell you about **adding**. We have to add up all the bugs we have collected so that Wizard Whimstaff does not think we are getting lazy. Can you help?

Task 1 Croak! Add each group of bugs to find the total. Wake us up when you are finished!

a ☐ + ☐ = ☐   e ☐ + ☐ = ☐

b ☐ + ☐ = ☐   f ☐ + ☐ = ☐

c ☐ + ☐ = ☐   g ☐ + ☐ = ☐

d ☐ + ☐ = ☐   h ☐ + ☐ = ☐

Task 2 You added the bugs really well. But can you count spiders? Have a try while we have a nap.

a ☐ + ☐ = ☐   b ☐ + ☐ = ☐

c ☐ + ☐ = ☐   d ☐ + ☐ = ☐

Task 3 Brain cell alert! Can you add numbers without pictures to help you? Try these sums.

a 9 + 3 =   b 12 + 5 =   c 7 + 11 =

d 5 + 9 =   e 13 + 7 =   f 24 + 4 =

Sorcerer's Skill Check

Burp! We have had a really good nap now. Show us what you have learned! Fill in the missing numbers.

a 7 + ☐ = 10   e 20 + ☐ = 24

b 12 + ☐ = 17   f 17 + ☐ = 27

c 16 + ☐ = 20   g 8 + ☐ = 19

d 9 + ☐ = 22   h 14 + ☐ = 25

My head hurts just watching your adding skills! Take another silver shield!

Silly Subtraction

Now you must learn about **subtraction**. That means **take away** sums, where you take one number away from another.

10 − 7 = 3 is a subtraction.
We have taken 7 away from 10.

You can check your answer by adding the answer to the number you took away. They should add up to the number you started with.

10 − 7 = 3. Add 7 to 3 and you get 10.

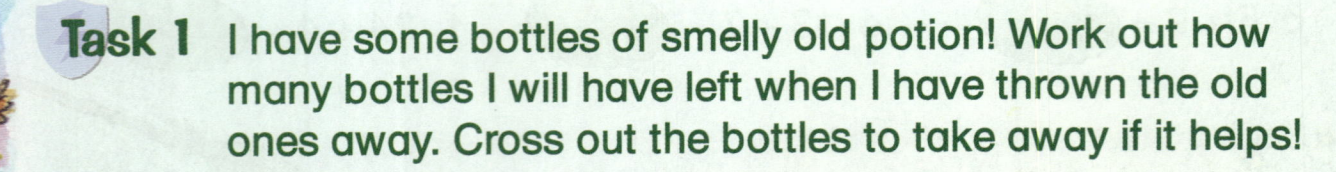

Task 1 I have some bottles of smelly old potion! Work out how many bottles I will have left when I have thrown the old ones away. Cross out the bottles to take away if it helps!

a − 7 = ☐

b − 9 = ☐

c − 4 = ☐

Task 2 Excellent! Now try these sums, young apprentice.

a 10 − 5 = ☐   b 10 − 2 = ☐   c 10 − 6 = ☐

d 10 − 3 = ☐   e 10 − 9 = ☐   f 10 − 8 = ☐

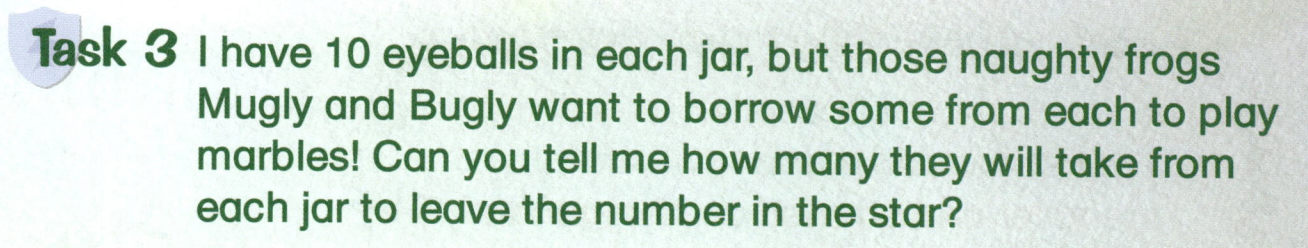

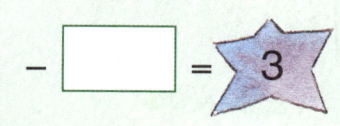

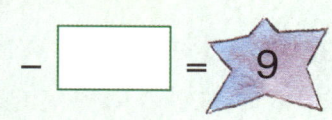

Task 3 I have 10 eyeballs in each jar, but those naughty frogs Mugly and Bugly want to borrow some from each to play marbles! Can you tell me how many they will take from each jar to leave the number in the star?

a ◯ − ☐ = ⭐ 6   d ◯ − ☐ = ⭐ 8

b ◯ − ☐ = ⭐ 3   e ◯ − ☐ = ⭐ 2

c ◯ − ☐ = ⭐ 9   f ◯ − ☐ = ⭐ 1

Sorcerer's Skill Check

One final task to check that you have learnt how to use subtraction magic. Write the answers in the boxes.

a 10 − ☐ = 7   d 10 − ☐ = 4

b 10 − ☐ = 3   e 10 − ☐ = 8

c 10 − ☐ = 5   f 10 − ☐ = 10

Croak! Well done, you saved us some work! Grab another silver shield while we grab a snooze.

Super Sizes

Oh dear!
I get so muddled about which things are **taller and shorter**, and **bigger and smaller**! It makes it hard to help Wizard Whimstaff tidy up the cave. He likes things arranged neatly on his shelves!

Task 1 Wizard Whimstaff has asked me to put these bottles in order, starting with the tallest and ending with the shortest. Can you help me by writing the correct order?

Task 2 You did well! Now can you help me put these things in order from the tallest to the shortest?

a

b

26

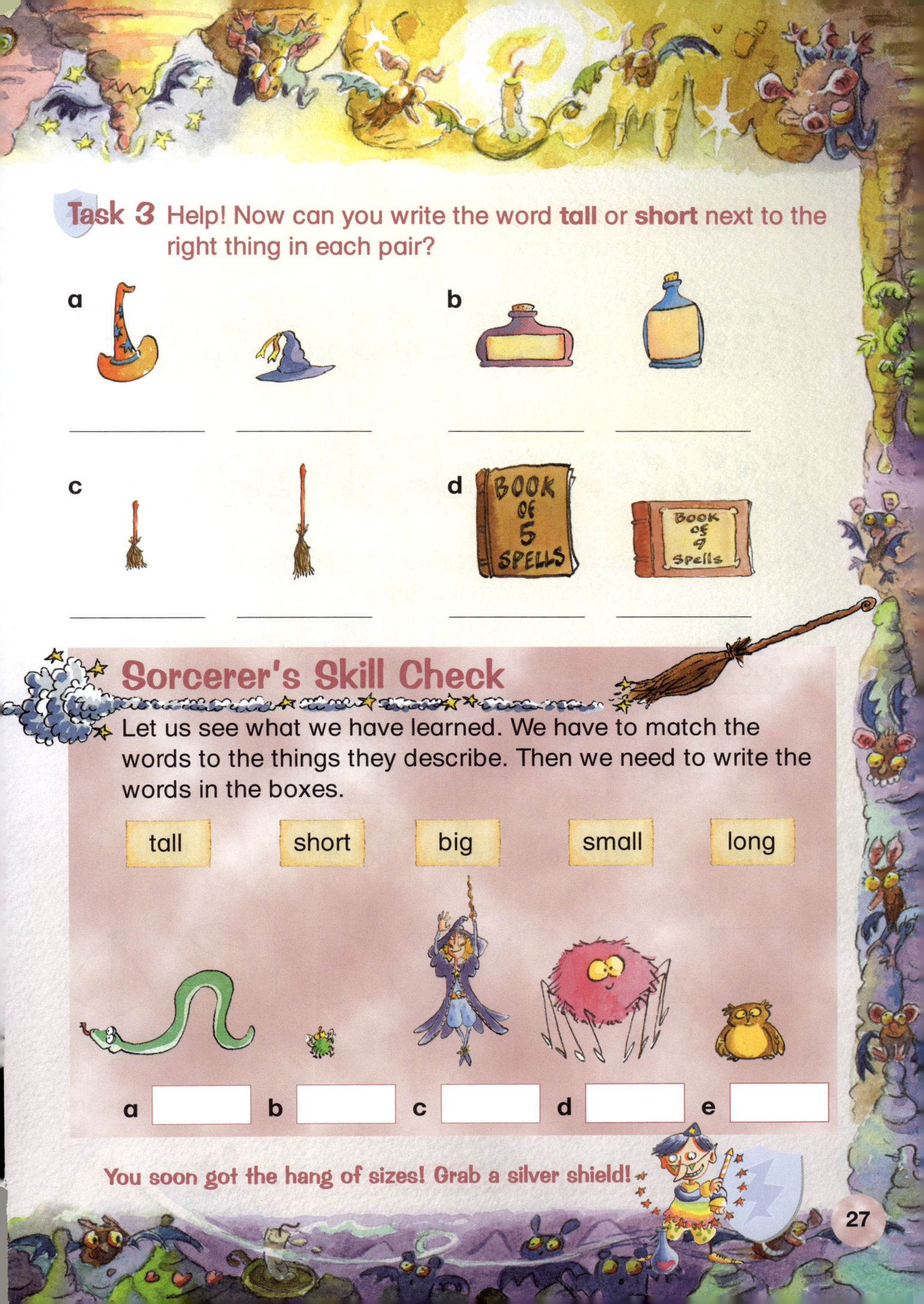

Task 3 Help! Now can you write the word **tall** or **short** next to the right thing in each pair?

a

b

c

d

Sorcerer's Skill Check

Let us see what we have learned. We have to match the words to the things they describe. Then we need to write the words in the boxes.

| tall | short | big | small | long |

a   b   c   d   e

You soon got the hang of sizes! Grab a silver shield!

Apprentice Wizard Challenge 2

Challenge 1 Match the bugs on the top row, to the bugs on the bottom row, to make pairs of ten.

a   b   c   d   e   f

Challenge 2 Each number has had doubling potion dropped on it. What number is made?

a double 5 = ☐

b double 4 = ☐

c double 3 = ☐

d double 2 = ☐

Challenge 3 Match the shapes to the names.

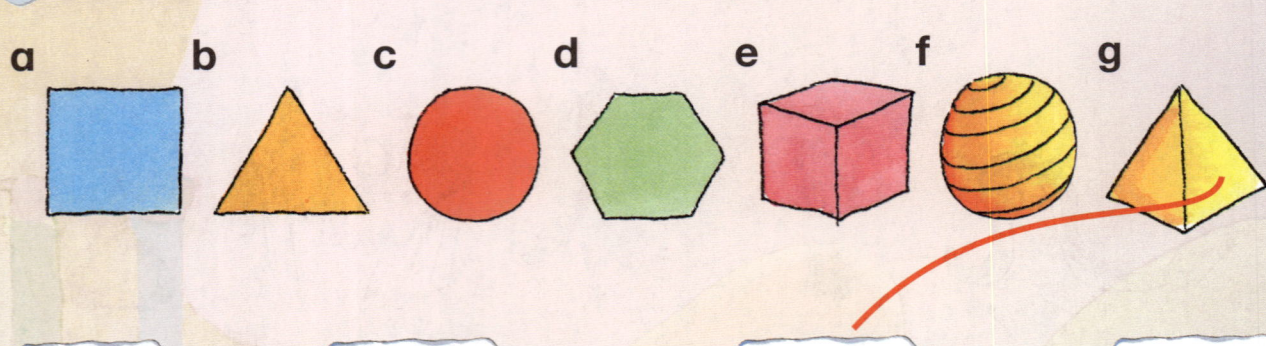

a   b   c   d   e   f   g

circle   triangle   pyramid   square

cube   hexagon   sphere

Challenge 4 Add the groups of bats to find the total.

a ☐ + ☐ = ☐   b ☐ + ☐ = ☐

c ☐ + ☐ = ☐   d ☐ + ☐ = ☐

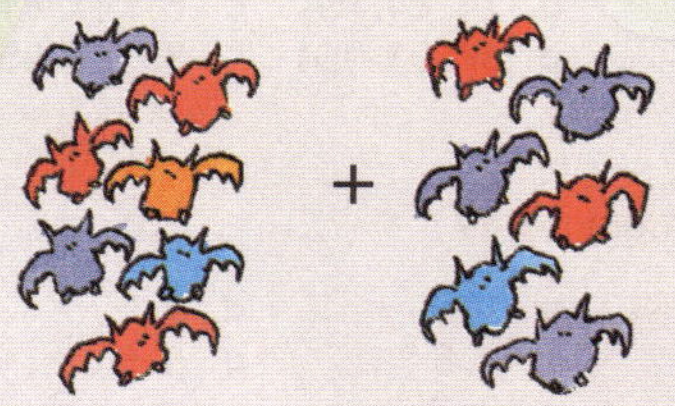

Challenge 5 Work out these subtractions.

a 10 − ☐ = 2   d 10 − ☐ = 1
b 10 − ☐ = 8   e 10 − ☐ = 7
c 10 − ☐ = 9   f 10 − ☐ = 4

Challenge 6 Put the things in order from the biggest to the smallest.

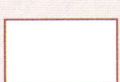

a  ☐ ☐ ☐

b  ☐ ☐ ☐

c ☐ ☐ ☐

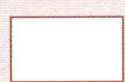

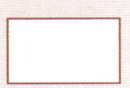

Put stars on the test tube to show your challenge score.
Then have the final shield for your trophy!

29

Answers

Pages 2–3

Task 1   a   7   b   12
          c   19

Task 2   a   9   b   11
          c   14

Task 3   a   8   d   20
          b   15   e   11
          c   14   f   19

Sorcerer's Skill Check
    a   10 butterflies   b   7 flies
    c   13 bugs

Pages 4–5

Task 1   a   1, 4, 7
          b   7, 8, 9, 11, 12, 13
          c   13, 14, 15, 16, 17, 18, 19

Task 2   a   4, 6, 7, 10, 11, 12, 13
          b   11, 13, 15, 17, 19
          c   2, 4, 6, 10, 11

Task 3   a   1, 2, 3, 4, 5, once I caught a bat alive!
          b   6, 7, 8, 9, 10 then I let her go again!
          c   1, 2, 3, 4, 5, then I caught a toad alive!
          d   6, 7, 8, 9, 10, then I let him go again!
          e   1, 2, Pointy made some stew,
          f   3, 4, I spilled it on the floor!
          g   5, 6, the Wizard did some tricks,
          h   7, 8, they were really great!

Sorcerer's Skill Check
    a   11, 12, 13, 14, 15
    b   8, 9, 12, 13
    c   13, 14, 15, 16, 17, 18
    d   3, 4, 5, 9, 10

Pages 6–7

Task 1   10, 20, 30, 40, 50, 60, 70, 80, 90, 100

Task 2   a   30, 40, 50, 60
          b   60, 70, 80, 90, 100
          c   70, 60, 50, 40

Task 3   Frogs in line 100 to 0.

Sorcerer's Skill Check
    Stars in a line with zero to 70 filled in.

Pages 8–9

Task 1   Frogs and pads joined: Zero and 0 joined with a line, one and 1 etc.

Task 2   a   1, one   d   4, four
          b   2, two   e   5, five
          c   3, three

Task 3   c, e, d, a, f, b

Task 4   a   ten   d   three
          b   one   e   six
          c   two

Sorcerer's Skill Check
    All numerals and words matched correctly.

Pages 10–11

Task 1   a   11   e   23
          b   15   f   30
          c   18   g   26
          d   20   h   21

Task 2   a   9   d   18
          b   13   e   28
          c   21   f   16

Task 3   a   16   d   10
          b   23   e   26
          c   29   f   18

Sorcerer's Skill Check
    a   28, 29, 30   d   12, 13, 14
    b   23, 24, 25   e   26, 27, 28
    c   10, 11, 12   f   16, 17, 18

Pages 12–13

Task 1   a   20   b   24
          c   42   d   59

Task 2   a   50   b   4
          c   87

Task 3   a   55   d   71
          b   84   e   76
          c   68   f   27

Sorcerer's Skill Check
    a   19, 29, 39   d   43, 53, 63
    b   24, 34, 44   e   77, 87, 97
    c   51, 61, 71   f   35, 45, 55

Pages 14–15

Challenge 1
    19 spiders

Challenge 2
    a   0, 1, 2, 3, 4, 5, 6, 7, 8, 9, 10
    b   11, 12, 13, 14, 15, 16, 17, 18, 19, 20

Challenge 3
    0, 10, 20, 30, 40, 50, 60, 70, 80, 90, 100

Challenge 4
    Check words and numerals are matched correctly.

Challenge 5
    a   28, 29, 30   d   12, 13, 14
    b   23, 24, 25   e   26, 27, 28
    c   10, 11, 12   f   16, 17, 18

Challenge 6
    a   39, 49, 59   d   45, 55, 65
    b   74, 84, 94   e   61, 71, 81
    c   81, 91, 101   f   35, 45, 55

Pages 16–17

Task 1   a   1, 9   d   4, 6
          b   2, 8   e   5, 5
          c   3, 7

Task 2   a   2, 8   d   1, 9
          b   3, 7   e   6, 4
          c   5, 5

Task 3   a   3, 7   d   8, 2
          b   0, 10   e   6, 4
          c   9, 1   f   5, 5

Sorcerer's Skill Check
    a   0 + 10 = 10   g   6 + 4 = 10
    b   1 + 9 = 10   h   7 + 3 = 10
    c   2 + 8 = 10   i   8 + 2 = 10
    d   3 + 7 = 10   j   9 + 1 = 10
    e   4 + 6 = 10   k   10 + 0 = 10
    f   5 + 5 = 10

Pages 18–19

Task 1   a   2   b   3
          c   4   d   1

Task 2   a   8   b   2
          c   4   d   6

Task 3   a   H   d   D
          b   H   e   D
          c   H   f   H

Sorcerer's Skill Check
    a   2   e   4
    b   4   f   3
    c   6   g   2
    d   8   h   1

Pages 20–21

Task 1   a   square   e   cube
          b   triangle   f   sphere
          c   circle   g   pyramid
          d   hexagon

Task 2   2 squares, 7 triangles, 7 circles

30

Task 3 Any picture containing 3 circles, 3 squares and 3 triangles.

Sorcerer's Skill Check
- a Triangle, 2D b Pyramid, 3D
- c Square, 2D

Pages 22–23

Task 1
- a 4 bugs + 6 bugs = 10
- b 4 bugs + 5 bugs = 9
- c 7 bugs + 6 bugs = 13
- d 3 bugs + 4 bugs = 7
- e 5 bugs + 6 bugs = 11
- f 3 bugs + 9 bugs = 12
- g 5 bugs + 3 bugs = 8
- h 8 bugs + 6 bugs = 14

Task 2
- a 8 spiders + 6 spiders = 14
- b 11 spiders + 5 spiders = 16
- c 7 spiders + 5 spiders = 12
- d 12 spiders + 3 spiders = 15

Task 3
- a 9 + 3 = 12   d 5 + 9 = 14
- b 12 + 5 = 17   e 13 + 7 = 20
- c 7 + 11 = 18   f 24 + 4 = 28

Sorcerer's Skill Check
- a 7 + 3 = 10   e 20 + 4 = 24
- b 12 + 5 = 17   f 17 + 10 = 27
- c 16 + 4 = 20   g 8 + 11 = 19
- d 9 + 13 = 22   h 14 + 11 = 25

Pages 24–25

Task 1
- a 3   b 1
- c 6

Task 2
- a 5   d 7
- b 8   e 1
- c 4   f 2

Task 3
- a 4   d 2
- b 7   e 8
- c 1   f 9

Sorcerer's Skill Check
- a 3   d 6
- b 7   e 2
- c 5   f 0

Pages 26–27

Task 1 e, c, b, a, d

Task 2
- a c, a, d, b   b a, c, b, d

Task 3
- a tall, short
- b short, tall
- c short, tall
- d tall, short

Sorcerer's Skill Check
- a long   d big
- b small   e short
- c tall

Pages 28–29

Challenge 1
- a 9, 1   d 4, 6
- b 0, 10   e 3, 7
- c 5, 5   f 2, 8

Challenge 2
- a 10   b 8
- c 6   d 4

Challenge 3
- a square   e cube
- b triangle f sphere
- c circle   g pyramid
- d hexagon

Challenge 4
- a 10   b 11
- c 13   d 9

Challenge 5
- a 10 − 8 = 2   d 10 − 9 = 1
- b 10 − 2 = 8   e 10 − 3 = 7
- c 10 − 1 = 9   f 10 − 6 = 4

Challenge 6
- a c, a, b   b c, a, b
- c c, b, a

The end

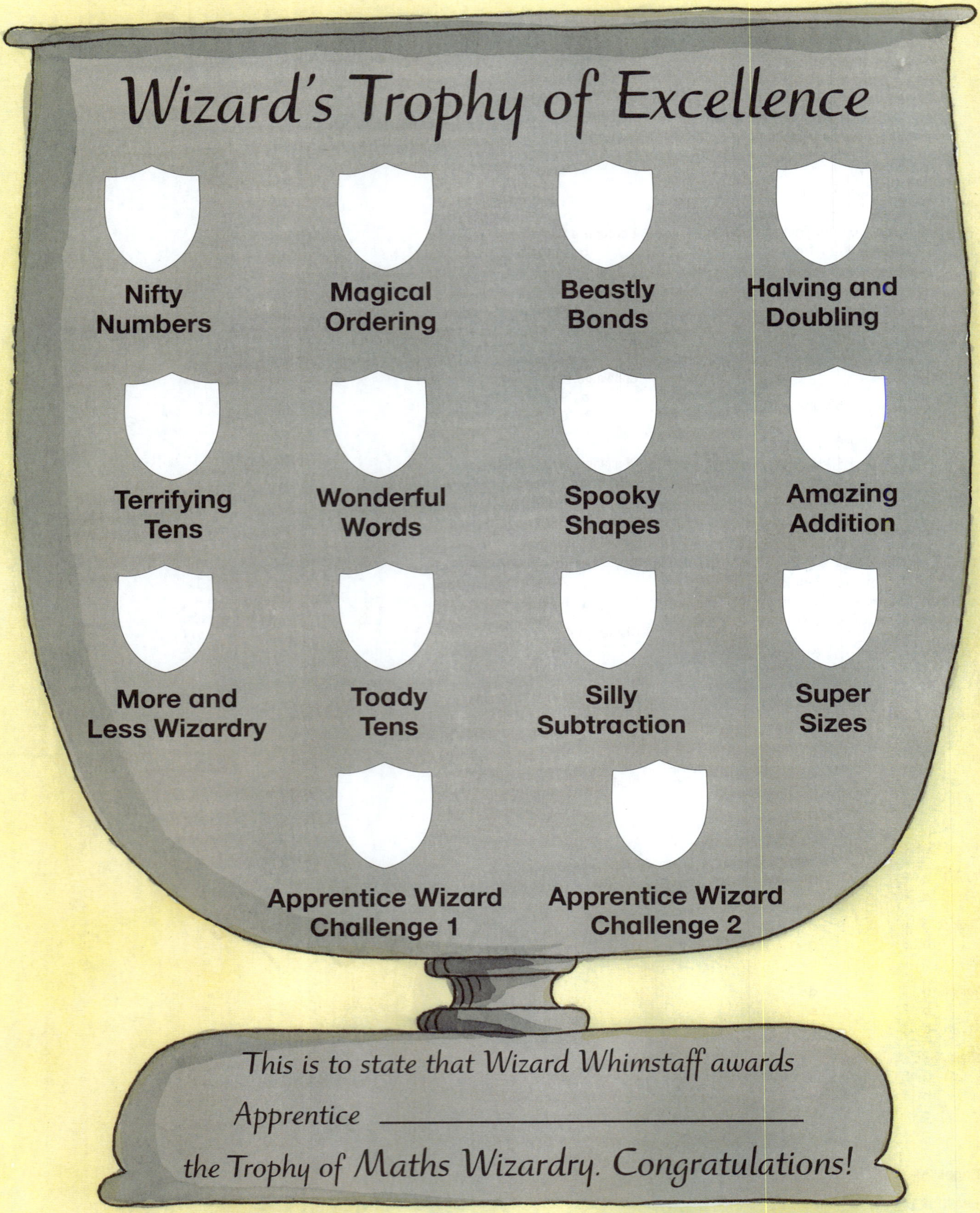

Wizard's Trophy of Excellence

Nifty Numbers	Magical Ordering	Beastly Bonds	Halving and Doubling
Terrifying Tens	Wonderful Words	Spooky Shapes	Amazing Addition
More and Less Wizardry	Toady Tens	Silly Subtraction	Super Sizes
	Apprentice Wizard Challenge 1	Apprentice Wizard Challenge 2	

This is to state that Wizard Whimstaff awards

Apprentice _____

the Trophy of Maths Wizardry. Congratulations!

Published 2002
07/270711

Published by Letts Educational
An imprint of HarperCollins*Publishers*
77–85 Fulham Palace Road
London W6 8JB
Phone orders: 0844 576 8126
Fax orders: 0844 576 8131
Email: education@harpercollins.co.uk
Website: www.lettsandlonsdale.com

Text © Lynn Huggins-Cooper
Design and illustrations © 2002 Letts Educational
Author: Lynn Huggins-Cooper
Book Concept and Development: Helen Jacobs and Sophie London
Series Editor: Lynn Huggins-Cooper

Design and Editorial: 2idesign ltd, Cambridge
Cover Design: Linda Males
Illustrations: Mike Phillips and Neil Chapman (Beehive Illustration)
Cover Illustration: Neil Chapman

All rights reserved. No part of this publication may be reproduced, stored in a retrieval system, or transmitted, in any form or by any means, electronic, mechanical, photocopying, recording or otherwise, without the prior permission of Letts Educational.

British Library Cataloguing in Publication Data
A CIP record for this book is available from the British Library.
ISBN 978-1-84315-123-4

Printed in China

Colour reproduction by PDQ Digital Media Solutions Limited, Bungay, Suffolk.